Hymn
and
Cocktail Sticks

Alan Bennett has been one of our leading dramatists since the success of *Beyond the Fringe* in the 1960s. His television series *Talking Heads* has become a modern-day classic, as have many of his works for stage including *Forty Years On*, *The Lady in the Van*, *A Question of Attribution*, *The Madness of George III* (together with the Oscar-nominated screenplay *The Madness of King George*), and an adaptation of Kenneth Grahame's *The Wind in the Willows*. At the National Theatre, London, *The History Boys* won numerous awards including *Evening Standard* and Critics' Circle awards for Best Play, an Olivier for Best New Play and the South Bank Award. On Broadway, *The History Boys* won five New York Drama Desk Awards, four Outer Critics' Circle Awards, a New York Drama Critics' Award, a New York Drama League Award and six Tonys. *The Habit of Art* opened at the National in 2009, and *People* in 2012. His collection of prose, *Untold Stories*, won the PEN/Ackerley Prize for autobiography, 2006. *The Uncommon Reader* was published in 2007 and *Smut: Two Unseemly Stories* in 2011.

ALAN BENNETT

Hymn
and
Cocktail Sticks

with introductions by the author

faber and faber

First published in 2012
by Faber and Faber Limited
74–77 Great Russell Street
London WC1B 3DA

The text of *Hymn* was first published by Faber and Faber Ltd
and Profile Books Ltd in *Untold Stories*, 2005.

Typeset by Country Setting, Kingsdown, Kent CT14 8ES
Printed in England by CPI Group (UK) Ltd, Croydon, CR0 4YY

A CIP record for this book is available from the British Library

978–0–571–29924–9

2 4 6 8 10 9 7 5 3 1

Contents

HYMN

Introduction

That I wrote *Hymn* is entirely thanks to the composer George Fenton, whom I've known since he appeared as a schoolboy in my first play *Forty Years On*, and who has written music for many of the plays since. In 2001 the Medici Quartet commissioned him to write a piece commemorating their thirtieth anniversary and he asked me to collaborate. *Hymn* was the result. First performed at the Harrogate Festival in August 2001, it is a series of memoirs with music. Besides purely instrumental passages for the quartet, many of the speeches are underscored, incorporating some of the hymns and music I remember from my childhood and youth.

At the first performance, in a later one at the Buxton Festival plus the live recording we made for the BBC, I played myself. Though I'd never appeared with musicians on a concert platform I didn't anticipate any difficulty. Having to memorise a script is what gives me stage fright, but here it was entirely in order to read the words; the musicians were reading from a score and so was I.

What I'd not anticipated was how in a concert situation the narrator is just one element in the composition, with timing to some extent taken out of his or her hands. There was a moment in the first performance when I stood up for my first speech, saw George cue me in and thought, just for a split second, 'If I don't speak now the whole thing falls apart.' I did speak, though my hesitation was enough to make it a slightly rough passage. It was enough, too, to make me more nervous than I had been . . . which was probably a good thing. That apart, the performance went off well. It was on the stage of the Royal Hall in Harrogate, an auditorium designed by the Edwardian theatre architect Frank Matcham and a riot of exuberant plasterwork. This was in August 2001. Ten days later the roof fell in and the theatre was closed for the next five years.

Never having worked with a string quartet before, rehearsals for me were something of an eye-opener. What astonished me was the freedom with which members of the quartet felt entitled to comment on each other's performances, speaking up when they felt one or other of them was too loud, say, or not incisive enough, comments which the player in question either took in good part or which provoked a reasoned defence. At no point, though, did I detect any animosity.

At first I explained this to myself by thinking that this particular quartet had been playing together for thirty years and it was familiarity, bred out of friendship and working together, that made them so magnanimous and forgiving. But no, I was told; string quartets and chamber music groups in general were most often like this.

I kept thinking of actors in a comparable situation where, should one actor venture to criticise or comment on the performance of a colleague, it would provoke resentment and sulks and certainly an appeal to the director. If an actor does have any opinions to offer on another actor's performance, the etiquette, the ironclad etiquette, is that such comments should be made to the director, who will then relay them to the actor in question in the form of direction and with no hint as to their source. Actors, one is always told, need to be loved. Quartet players are seemingly thicker skinned.

Of course I am not the first to have noted the musicians' resilience, and indeed the string quartet has been used as a model in business schools to exemplify a readiness to accept constructive criticism without hurt feelings. What players do quarrel about, if they ever do, I'm not sure.

It has always been a mystery to me how it was my father came to learn the violin, though, like so many things about my parents' early life, I never thought to ask him while I still could. It's an unrewarding instrument for a beginner, the more so in his case because he received scant encouragement at home. His mother died when he was a child, leaving his father with four sons to bring up. He quickly married again, this time a sour-faced woman, a stalwart of the chapel whose name I have never known as she was always referred to in the family as 'The Gimmer', a gimmer being a sheep that has had no lambs. Though my father was allowed to practise the violin in the front room, it was only by the light of the street lamp that came in through the window. But still he persisted, perhaps knowing that he had perfect pitch and could name the notes if he heard someone else playing.

How he knew so much orchestral music is another question I never asked him. If there were orchestral concerts in Leeds when he was a young man I doubt that he could have afforded to go, and it would have been with his first and only girlfriend, my mother, and she never mentioned it. Brass bands are a possibility and it's true some of the music he knew – *Poet and Peasant, Ruy Blas* and Rossini's *Semiramide* – was the kind of showpiece stuff that bands went in for. It was only in middle age that my parents would have had a wireless, when he started playing along to that.

As time went on it became increasingly difficult to question him about the past as he took the interrogation to mean he was coming to the end of his life, which at that time he wasn't, his relatively early death wholly unexpected. Still, remembering what a struggle he'd had to acquire his skill, it must have been galling when he tried to pass it on to my brother and me how unserious we were about it and how reluctant to practise. He had practised with no encouragement at all; his pampered sons couldn't even be bothered. 'Now the Day is Over' isn't a hymn one hears very often nowadays, but if ever I do it transports me to the attic at 92A Otley Road where I am scraping it out on the half-size violin.

These days, though, hymns are changing. Gone are the days when I could sing them without looking at the book. The standards these days – 'Make Me a Channel of Thy Peace', 'Amazing Grace' and 'Lord of the Dance' – have me glued to the hymn book and not all that sure of the tune. Even with the old standards – 'Praise My Soul the King of Heaven', 'O Worship the King' – they've sometimes been amended to suit the taste of the time and it's like missing a step on the stair.

Hubberholme, the church at the very tip of the West Riding where *Hymn* finishes up, isn't an especially beautiful church inside, scraped as so many churches were in the nineteenth century and the plaster taken off to reveal the unlovely stonework underneath. Still, it has its rood loft and a nice atmosphere. It also has pews made by Thompson of Kilburn, the famous Mouse Man, and on the occasions when I've called at the church to look at the rood loft the only other visitors have been Thompson fans scouring the pews for the trademark mouse. They never give the rood loft a second glance, making me feel somewhat superior, though between Larkin's 'ruin-bibber, randy for antique' and the mouse-hunters I don't suppose there's much to choose.

There are different ways of being English. Churches don't come into it much these days and that they're so often unregarded for me augments their appeal. Since I seldom attend a service this could be thought hypocrisy. But that's not un-English either.

Alan Bennett, October 2012

Hymn with music by George Fenton premiered at the Harrogate International Festival in August 2001. Alan Bennett played himself and the music was performed by the Medici Quartet:

Paul Robertson (*violin*), Stephen Morris (*violin*), Ivo-Jan van der Werff (*viola*), Anthony Lewis (*cello*)

It was revived in the Lyttelton auditorium of the National Theatre, London, on 22 November 2012:

Alan Bennett Alex Jennings

and performed by three string quartets drawn from members of the Southbank Sinfonia:

QUARTET 1
Judith Choi Castro (*violin*), Barbara Zdziarska (*violin*), Kimberly Jill Harrenstein (*viola*), Ivan Leon / Arthur Boutillier (*cello*)

QUARTET 2
Minsi Yang (*violin*), Seila Tammisola (*violin*), Jenny Wilkinson (*viola*), Alisa Liubarskaya (*cello*)

QUARTET 3
Gaëlle-Anne Michel (*violin*), Aisling Manning (*violin*), Lisa Bucknell (*viola*), Arthur Boutillier (*cello*)

Director Nadia Fall
Designer Bob Crowley
Lighting Designer Tom Snell
Sound Designer Mike Walker
Producer Pádraig Cusack

> And so through all the length of days,
> Thy goodness faileth never.
> Good shepherd may I sing thy praise
> Within thy house forever.

Up the words come, unbidden, known but never learned.
Some of that weightless baggage carried down the years,
not from piety or belief, and more credentials than creed,
a testimonial that I am one of those boys state-educated
in the forties and fifties who came by the words of
Hymns Ancient and Modern through singing them day in
day out at school every morning in assembly.

It's a dwindling band; old-fashioned and of a certain age,
you can pick us out at funerals and memorial services,
because we can sing the hymns without the book.

> Alleluia alleluia,
> Hearts to heaven and voices raised,
> Sing to God a hymn of gladness
> Sing to God a hymn of praise.

With me, there are hymns at home, too, because my
father is an amateur violinist and on Sunday nights plays
along to the music on the wireless, warming up with
Albert Sandler and his Palm Court Orchestra then taking
off with the hymn singing on *Sunday Half Hour.*

So hymns are him playing his fiddle. At one period Dad's
thoughts turn to something larger than the violin and he
invests in a double bass, thinking to augment his butcher's
wages by working nights as a player in a dance band.
One of the several burdens of wives are the hare-brained

schemes of husbands, and my mother was never other than sceptical of my father's money-making enterprises. Another had been the manufacture of home-made herb beer. This was referred to by Mam as 'taking on Tetleys' and the double bass period as 'your Dad's Geraldo phase'.

It means, though, that as a change from *Sunday Half Hour* the family are now mustered round the wireless and made to listen to Henry Hall and the Andrews Sisters.

Mares eat oats and does eat oats and little lambs eat ivy, A kid'll eat ivy too, wouldn't you? Pom pom.

'Did you hear that?' Dad would say. 'That's the bass giving the beat! That'll be me!' It was difficult to enthuse.

To no one's surprise, he never got far with the bass. Quite literally, as they often wouldn't let him even put it on the tram. And just as the home-made beer saga had ended in the explosion of half a dozen bottles that practically wrecked the scullery, so the double bass era ended with a succession of rows with tram conductors after which Dad reverted to the violin.

> Praise to the holiest in the height
> And in the depths be praise.
> In all his works most wonderful,
> Most sure in all his ways.

The words are those of Cardinal Newman's hymn but they are also part of Elgar's *Dream of Gerontius*, heard first in Leeds Town Hall in 1952. I thought Elgar had missed a trick by not using the familiar tune and at its first outing in 1900 the audience had thought so too, with the general feeling then that this sublime work was a bit of a dud.

Most of my musical education was in Leeds Town Hall at weekly concerts by the short-lived (but to me always memorable) Yorkshire Symphony Orchestra. They excelled in English music – Delius particularly, whom I was astonished to find had been born in Bradford. And George Butterworth, too, from York, who died on the Somme in 1916.

The cheapest seats and the school seats were behind the orchestra and here the double bass raises its ponderous voice again as our chosen perch was behind the basses. It was rather like watching the circus from behind the elephants. Hardly a lyrical instrument, the bass tends to attract players of a like disposition, dogged and even disenchanted with a robust no-nonsense approach to performance. Indifferent to applause, if we go on too long at the end of a concert, the principal, a Mr Campbell, turns round and says, 'Have you no homes to go to?'

At that age, though, we find this work-a-day attitude to music-making infectious. Sitting looking down on the conductor, we fifteen-year-olds are alert to pretension and subject the sometimes eminent musicians to our sceptical schoolboy scrutiny, grading them by the degree of their self-regard.

It isn't just a matter of histrionics with the baton, as both Barbirolli and Sargent, for instance, go in for a good deal of that, but they are not the same. Urbane, Brylcreemed and always with a carnation in his buttonhole and a wolfish smile, Sir Malcolm is an obvious showman. Sir John, unkempt and in a rumpled tail-coat with his bow tie on the skew and sometimes without his bottom teeth, seems entirely unselfconscious, but he is a showman too – both of them putting on a performance. For me, always a sucker for the unassuming, it is Barbirolli who touches the heart and serves the music, unlike Sargent, who merely presents it.

So it is not just music that I learn, sitting on those harsh benches, Saturday by Saturday. Music in the concert hall is also a moral education, and watching the musicians at close quarters I realise that it is not just ecstasy and inspiration but that there is drudge to it too. Sometimes, the players would be on the same tram coming home, and I see that they are just like everybody else – shabby, in dirty raincoats and sometimes with tab ends in their mouths; ordinary people who, half an hour ago, were artists and agents of the sublime.

That music had nothing to do with showing off was, I see now, one of the lessons my father had been wanting me to learn when I was ten years old when he tried to teach me the violin. He knew instinctively that art has not much to do with artistic, and that there was no need for a lot of carry-on, or, as Dad always put it, 'a lot of splother'.

His violin case is deceptively ordinary, battered even, and kept in my parents' bedroom, which is where my father generally does his practice. Having made sure that he is out, I lay the case on the bed, unflip its two catches and open the lid to reveal, snugly couched in velvet, this glowing tawny thing. It is like coming on a newly fallen horse chestnut, the neat housing split to reveal the conker's wet gleam. I stroke the coved back, grained as if with spine and ribs, hold the scrolled head in my hand and feel its weight, running my fingers round the piped and scalloped edge and peering through the S-shaped holes into its dark interior.

Mounted on the underside of the lid is the bow and that too is finely done, the handle inlaid with mother-of-pearl, the end tipped with ivory; so pampered this instrument seems to me to be, so lavishly appointed, with nothing spared for its protection and comfort, that even my looking has to be hurried and furtive, knowing that if my father catches me at it, I shall be in trouble. 'It's not a toy.' But I don't think of it as a toy either. It is the most luxurious object in the house, and sensitive to the spell it casts, I see myself playing it – even pretend to, in front of the dressing-table mirror.

So I ask to learn. I'm a clever boy. I am sure it will not be hard.

'To begin with, you don't hold it like that, you hold it like this.' He takes the bow out of my ten-year-old hand. 'Just do it naturally.' He bends my fingers round the handle of the bow, covering my hands with his big butcher's hands, standing there in his shirtsleeves and shop trousers and smelling of meat. We are in the hot attic under the roof with the half-size violin I have to learn on, nothing like as glamorous as his, a chipped, unpolished brown little thing that looks as though it can't produce a note.

'You're holding the bow wrong again. Nobody holds it like that. People will laugh at you.' He purses my fingers again round the bow handle, his own violin held casually under his chin, jutting out from his shoulder as he tightens the silky hair of the bow. Even at ten, I know this is showing off, 'Look! No hands!' the kindest labelling of it. But holding this scrolled extension of himself is also him being a man and doing something that with my puny neck and chin I know I can't do now and probably ever.

'I've written you on the notes: E, G, B, D, F. What do they stand for?' This, at least, I know. Every Good Boy Deserves Favour. I know it too, because this favoured boy is not just an aid to memory but to me almost a creature of flesh and blood. It is as if the very structure of the stave has been rigged against me and this good boy deserving of favour is all the things I am not – capable, modest and quiet, who holds the bow with his small fingers just as my father does in his big ones and does not scrape it agonisingly across the strings as I do, but extracts from this unpromising almost plywood fiddle something sweet and tuneful. This good boy, who is not me, deserves favour from my father, as I never shall.

Violin still jutting, Dad puts a sheet of music on the gunmetal stand. 'Now the Day is Over', copied out from *Hymns Ancient and Modern* in a hand as square and blunt as his fingers.

> Now the day is over,
> Night is drawing nigh.
> Shadows of the evening
> Steal across the sky.

I start on the first note, dragging the bow across the strings.

'Nay, Alan! Frame yourself. Look at your fingers!' Once again, his big butcher's hands come over mine, gripping the bow for me, so that now it is he who is playing the tune, not me. I let go of the violin and it falls on the floor.

'You dateless article! What is the point?' At first, I think that he is going to hit me, but, golden violin in one hand and bow in the other, he can't, and instead he charges off down the attic steps. I know that I am a disappointment to my father and that this disappointment will outlast the violin and my childhood and go down into the grave.

The attic door bangs shut. Through the open skylight I hear the trams hurtling down Otley Road and the bell-ringers over at St Chad's beginning their practice. I climb up on the chair and look out at the evening sky.

I've always liked looking in churches and though I'm not quite one of those who, in Philip Larkin's words, 'tap and jot and know what rood lofts were', I do know what rood lofts were and it has brought me to Hubberholme at the top of Wharfedale and the very tip of the West Riding.

The church is broad and low, like its liturgy, I imagine, but unique in the West Riding – its rood loft survives. Put up in 1558, it was perhaps salvaged from Coverham Abbey and brought over the tops on a farm cart. But they were behind the times at Hubberholme. They did not know in 1558 that Catholic Queen Mary was dead and that, as they were putting up their loft, everywhere else the lofts were coming down. But amazingly it survives and is still here and a proper loft it is too, slatted as it could be for hay and straw as much as for candles and the cross.

Centuries pass – births, marriages and deaths – the church's next moment in history recorded in a picture frame hung slightly askew on one of the pillars – a roll of honour with the names and, unusually for England, the photographs of the young men of the parish who died in the First War.

The harvest in, they go off on a farm cart, too, probably, down the dale to join those queuing to enlist outside Skipton Town Hall. And four years later, in Wilfred Owen's words:

> A few, a few, too few for drums and yells,
> May creep back, silent, to village wells
> Up half-known roads.

And once a year they form up again and in that annual official pause in a silence here where it is always silent they recall the lost friends and comrades pictured in the church.

One who does come back from that war, and years later has his ashes scattered here, is J. B. Priestley, and on another pillar is a plaque to say so.

The rood, the roll of honour, the ashes of a writer – the remnants of history, the random trig points of time.

I have never found it easy to belong. So much repels. Hymns help. They blur. And here among the tombs and tablets and vases of dead flowers, and lists of the fallen, it is less hard to feel, at least, tacked on to church and country.

Amen. Or, with that lilting interrogation with which young people nowadays cast doubt on any certainty, Amen?

HYMN

with music by
GEORGE FENTON

Hymn I

The King of Love my Shepherd is

George Fenton

The Quartet on stage tunes up. The cello introduction
carries straight on, as though he is still checking his tuning.

Alan Bennett
And so through all the length of days,

Thy goodness faileth never. / Good shepherd may I sing thy
praise / Within thy house forever.

Up the words come, unbidden, known but never learned.

Some of that weightless baggage carried down the years, not

from piety or belief, and more credentials than creed, a
testimonial that I am one of those boys state-educated in the

forties and fifties who came by the words of *Hymns Ancient*

and Modern through singing them day in day out at school
every morning in assembly.

It's a dwindling band; old-fashioned and of a certain age, you
can pick us out at funerals and memorial services, because we
can sing the hymns without the book.

> Alleluia alleluia,
> Hearts to heaven and voices raised,
> Sing to God a hymn of gladness
> Sing to God a hymn of praise.

Hymn II

Palm Court

George Fenton

With me, there are hymns at home, too, because my father is an amateur violinist and on Sunday nights plays along to the music on the wireless, warming up with Albert Sandler and his

Palm Court Orchestra then taking off with the hymn singing on *Sunday Half Hour*.

So hymns are him playing
his fiddle.

Hymn III

includes a quote from Mairzy Doats

George Fenton

At one period Dad's thoughts turn to something larger than the violin and he invests in a double bass, thinking to augment his butcher's wages by working nights as a player in a dance band.

One of the several burdens of wives are the hare-brained schemes of husbands, and my mother was never other than sceptical of my father's money-making enterprises. Another

had been the manufacture of home-made herb beer. This was

referred to by Mam as 'taking on Tetleys' and the double bass

period as 'your Dad's Geraldo phase'. It means, though, that as a change from *Sunday Half Hour* the family are now

mustered round the wireless and made to listen to Henry Hall and the Andrews Sisters.

Mares eat oats and does eat

oats and little lambs eat ivy, / A kid'll eat ivy too, wouldn't you? Pom pom pom.

'Did you hear that?' Dad would say. 'That's the bass giving the beat! That'll be me!' It was difficult to enthuse.

To no one's surprise, he never got far with the bass. Quite literally, as they often wouldn't let him even put it on the tram. And just as the home-made beer saga had ended in the explosion of half a dozen bottles that practically wrecked the scullery, so the double bass era ended with a succession of rows with tram conductors after which Dad reverted to the violin.

Hymn IV
Dream of Gerontius

ELGAR
arr. George Fenton

Praise to the holiest in the height / And in the depths be praise.
In all his works most wonderful, / Most sure in all his ways.

The words are those of Cardinal Newman's hymn but they are

also part of Elgar's *Dream of Gerontius*, heard first in Leeds Town Hall in 1952.

I thought Elgar had missed a trick by not using the familiar tune and at its first outing in 1900 the audience had thought so too, with the general feeling then that this sublime work was a bit of a dud.

Most of my musical education was in Leeds Town Hall at weekly concerts by the short-lived (but to me always memorable) Yorkshire Symphony Orchestra. They excelled in English music – Delius particularly, whom I was astonished to find had been born in Bradford. And George Butterworth, too, from York, who died on the Somme in 1916.

The cheapest seats and the school seats were behind the orchestra and here the double bass raises its ponderous voice again as our chosen perch was behind the basses. It was rather like watching the circus from behind the elephants.

Hardly a lyrical instrument, the bass tends to attract players of a like disposition, dogged and even disenchanted with a robust no-nonsense approach to performance. Indifferent to applause, if we go on too long at the end of a concert, the principal, a Mr Campbell, turns round and says, 'Have you no homes to go to?'

Hymn V

Fantastic Dance

DELIUS
arr. George Fenton

At that age, though, we find this work-a-day attitude to music-

making infectious. Sitting looking down on the conductor, we

fifteen-year-olds are alert to pretension and subject the
sometimes eminent musicians to our sceptical schoolboy

scrutiny, grading them by the degree of their self-regard.

It isn't just a matter of histrionics with the baton, as both Barbirolli and Sargent, for instance, go in for a good deal of that, but they are not the same. Urbane, Brylcreemed and always with a carnation in his buttonhole and a wolfish smile,

Sir Malcolm is an obvious showman. Sir John, unkempt and in a rumpled tail-coat with his bow tie on the skew and sometimes without his bottom teeth, seems entirely unselfconscious, but

he is a showman too – both of them putting on a performance. For me, always a sucker for the unassuming, it is Barbirolli

who touches the heart and serves the music, unlike Sargent, who merely presents it. So it is not just music that I learn, sitting on those harsh benches, Saturday by Saturday. Music in

the concert hall is also a moral education, and watching the musicians at close quarters I realise that it is not just ecstasy and inspiration but that there is drudge to it too. Sometimes, the players would be on the same tram coming home, and I see

that they are just like everybody else – shabby, in dirty raincoats and sometimes with tab ends in their mouths; ordinary people who, half an hour ago, were artists and agents of the sublime.

That music had nothing to do with showing off was, I see now, one of the lessons my father had been wanting me to learn when I was ten years old when he tried to teach me the violin. He knew instinctively that art has not much to do with artistic, and that there was no need for a lot of carry-on, or, as Dad always put it, 'a lot of splother'.

Hymn VI

His violin case is deceptively ordinary, battered even, and kept in my parents' bedroom, which is where my father generally does his practice. Having made sure that he is out, I lay the

case on the bed, unflip its two catches and open the lid to reveal, snugly couched in velvet, this glowing tawny thing. It is like coming on a newly fallen horse chestnut, the neat housing

split to reveal the conker's wet gleam. I stroke the coved back, grained as if with spine and ribs, hold the scrolled head in my

hand and feel its weight, running my fingers round the piped

and scalloped edge and peering through the S-shaped holes into
its dark interior.

Mounted on the underside of the lid is the bow and that too is
finely done, the handle inlaid with mother-of-pearl, the end
tipped with ivory; so pampered this instrument seems to me to

be, so lavishly appointed, with nothing spared for its protection and comfort, that even my looking has to be hurried and furtive, knowing that if my father catches me at it, I shall be in trouble.

'It's not a toy.' But I don't think of it as a toy either. It is the most luxurious object in the house, and sensitive to the spell it

casts, I see myself playing it – even pretend to, in front of the dressing-table mirror. So I ask to learn. I'm a clever boy. I am sure it will not be hard.

Hymn VII

EGBDF

George Fenton

'To begin with, you don't hold it like that, you hold it like this.'
He takes the bow out of my ten-year-old hand. 'Just do it
naturally.' He bends my fingers round the handle of the bow,

covering my hands with his big butcher's hands, standing there
in his shirtsleeves and shop trousers and smelling of meat. We
are in the hot attic under the roof with the half-size violin

I have to learn on, nothing like as glamorous as his, a chipped, unpolished brown little thing that looks as though it can't produce a note.

'You're holding the bow wrong again. Nobody holds it like that. People will laugh at you.' He purses my fingers again

round the bow handle, his own violin held casually under his chin, jutting out from his shoulder as he tightens the silky hair of the bow. Even at ten, I know this is showing off.

'Look! No hands!' the kindest labelling of it. But holding this scrolled extension of himself is also him being a man and doing

something that with my puny neck and chin I know I can't do now and probably ever.

'I've written you on the notes: E, G, B, D, F. What do they stand for?' This, at least, I know. Every Good Boy Deserves

Favour. I know it too, because this favoured boy is not just an

aid to memory but to me almost a creature of flesh and blood.
It is as if the very structure of the stave has been rigged against

me and this good boy deserving of favour is all the things I am
not – capable, modest and quiet, who holds the bow with his
small fingers just as my father does in his big ones and does
not scrape it agonisingly across the strings as I do, but extracts

from this unpromising almost plywood fiddle something sweet and tuneful.

This good boy, who is not me, deserves favour from my father, as I never shall.

Violin still jutting, Dad puts a sheet of music on the gunmetal stand.

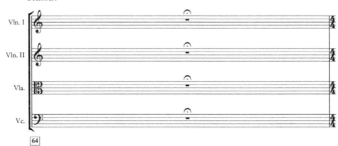

'Now the Day is Over', copied out from *Hymns Ancient and Modern* in a hand as square and blunt as his fingers.

Now the day is over, / Night is drawing nigh.

Shadows of the evening / Steal across the sky.

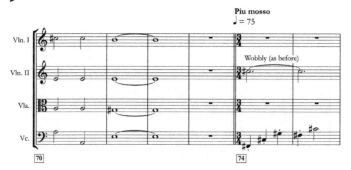

I start on the first note, dragging the bow across the strings. 'Nay, Alan! Frame yourself. Look at your fingers!' Once again,

his big butcher's hands come over mine, gripping the bow for me, so that now it is he who is playing the tune, not me.

I let go of the violin and it falls on the floor.

'You dateless article! What is the point?' At first, I think that he is going to hit me, but, golden violin in one hand and bow in the other, he can't, and instead he charges off down the attic steps. I know that I am a disappointment to my father and that this disappointment will outlast the violin and my childhood and go down into the grave.

The attic door bangs shut. Through the open skylight I hear the trams hurtling down Otley Road and the bell-ringers over at St Chad's beginning their practice. I climb up on the chair and look out at the evening sky.

Hymn VIII
Interlude

George Fenton

I've always liked looking in churches and though I'm not quite one of those who, in Philip Larkin's words, 'tap and jot and know what rood lofts were', I do know what rood lofts were and it has brought me to Hubberholme at the top of Wharfedale and the very tip of the West Riding.

The church is broad and low, like its liturgy, I imagine, but unique in the West Riding – its rood loft survives. Put up in 1558, it was perhaps salvaged from Coverham Abbey and brought over the tops on a farm cart. But they were behind the times at Hubberholme. They did not know in 1558 that Catholic Queen Mary was dead and that, as they were putting up their loft, everywhere else the lofts were coming down. But amazingly it survives and is still here and a proper loft it is too, slatted as it could be for hay and straw as much as for candles and the cross.

Centuries pass – births, marriages and deaths – the church's next moment in history recorded in a picture frame hung slightly askew on one of the pillars – a roll of honour with the names and, unusually for England, the photographs of the young men of the parish who died in the First War.

The harvest in, they go off on a farm cart, too, probably, down the dale to join those queuing to enlist outside Skipton Town Hall.

Hymn IX
Amen

George Fenton

And four years later, in Wilfred Owen's words: A few, a few, too few for drums and yells, / May creep back, silent, to village wells / Up half-known roads.

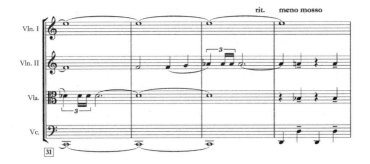

And once a year they form up again and in that annual official pause in a silence here where it is always silent they recall the lost friends and comrades pictured in the church.

One who does come back from that war, and years later has his ashes scattered here, is J. B. Priestley, and on another pillar is a plaque to say so.

The rood, the roll of honour, the ashes of a writer – the remnants of history, the random trig points of time.

I have never found it easy to belong. So much repels. Hymns help. They blur.

And here among the tombs and tablets and vases of dead

flowers, and lists of the fallen, it is less hard to feel, at least,
tacked on to church and country.

Amen.

Or, with that lilting interrogation with which young people
nowadays cast doubt on any certainty, Amen?

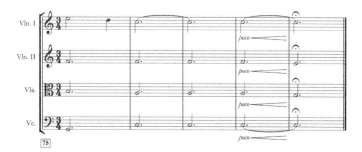

COCKTAIL STICKS

Introduction

From time to time at literary festivals and suchlike I do readings, mainly of extracts from my published diaries, which are generally followed by a question-and-answer session. One of the questions that regularly comes up is whether I have any misgivings or regrets about having written so much about my parents. 'No' is the short answer, and I certainly don't feel, as the questioner sometimes implies, that there is any need for apology. 'Why do you write about Yorkshire when half the time you don't live there?' is the question in a different form. 'Why do you write about your parents when they're no longer around?'

Distance is one answer – perspective. But I will often quote the American writer Flannery O'Connor who, in *Mystery and Manners* (1969) said that anyone who survives their childhood has enough material to last them the rest of their days.

But I don't quite see it like that either, as in my case (and this is partly what *Cocktail Sticks* is about) I had hardly written about them readily, and it took me a while before in a formal way I did, as my first volume of autobiography, *Writing Home*, wasn't published until 1994, while the second, *Untold Stories*, was ten years or so later. It's true that many of the TV plays I have written about the North owe a good deal to my parents' way of talking and looking at things, which is what my mother means when she remarks in *Cocktail Sticks*, 'By, I've given you some script!' But I don't think that is what the question implies, which is more that my parents were a shy and retiring couple, so to write about them even after their deaths is to violate their privacy, with autobiography a kind of betrayal. Not surprisingly, I don't buy this at all.

Both my parents felt constrained, even imprisoned, by their lack of education, though it was as much temperament that held them back. That needed talking about, it seemed to me, just as my mother's depression needed to be brought into the open, if only because this was a more common experience than is (or was then) generally admitted. That it seemed to me was no betrayal. And no betrayal to dramatise it either. And I'm not sure they wouldn't agree. Flannery O'Connor again: 'I once had the feeling I would dig my mother's grave with my writing, too, but I later discovered this was vanity on my part. They are hardier than we think.'

That said, it can be no fun having a writer in the family, always on the make, never happy to let things lie undescribed or leave them unremembered, and ready, too, to tweak experience if the drama or the narrative demands it. Philip Roth, keeping watch at his father's deathbed, knows that he is there out of affection but also because, as he admits, he will one day write about it. 'It is,' he says, 'an unseemly profession.'

Had I had any thoughts of 'being a writer' (which is not the same as writing), I would have been discouraged when I looked at my family, so ordinary did they seem and so empty the landscape. To be brought up in Leeds in the forties was to learn early on the quite useful lesson that life is generally something that happens elsewhere. True, I was around in time for the Second World War, but so far as Leeds was concerned that was certainly something that happened elsewhere. From time to time the sirens went and my brother and I were wrapped in blankets and hustled out to the air-raid shelter that stood outside our suburban front door, there to await the longed-for rain of bombs. Sheffield caught it, Liverpool caught it, but Leeds never. 'Why should it? I live here,' was my reasoning, though there was a more objective explanation. The city specialised in the manufacture of ready-made suits and the cultivation of rhubarb, and though the war aims of the German High Command were notoriously quixotic, I imagine a line had to be drawn somewhere. Thus in the whole course of hostilities very few bombs fell on Leeds and those that did were promptly torn apart by schoolboys starved of shrapnel.

All through the war there was a slogan painted on a wall in Wellington Street: 'Start the Second Front Now'. What this injunction meant I never knew at the time . . . It was still there in the early sixties, when it fell, as most things eventually do in Leeds, to the bulldozer. When with the invasion of Normandy the Second Front actually did start it still remained a mystery. We were told that particular day was D-Day and I'm not sure we weren't given a holiday, but I still managed to feel cheated. If this was D-Day, I reasoned that logically there must already have been an A-Day, a B-Day and a C-Day, and me being me and Leeds being Leeds we had, of course, missed them. I note at the age of ten a fully developed ability not quite to enjoy myself, a capacity I have retained intact ever since. I think this is one of the things that *Cocktail Sticks* is about.

It's also about finding something to write about. As I've said, childhood is always high on a writer's list but in the 1940s it was as if childhood itself was on the ration, dull, without frills and done up like the groceries of the time in plain utility packets. We were not well off but nor were we poor, and we were, I imagine, happy. Home – and this is *Cocktail Sticks* – was nothing to write home about. Larkin says that they fuck you up, your mum and dad. And if you end up writing, then that's fine because if they have, then you've got something to write about. But if they haven't fucked you up, you don't have anything to write about, so then they've fucked you up good and proper.

Leeds at that time was an almost wholly nineteenth-century city which, like most northern cities before the clean air campaign, was black as soot. Growing up, I could see some of its Victorian grandeur, but I was like Hector in *The History Boys*, 'famished for antiquity'. As a boy in a provincial city I was famished for celebrity too and famished, if the truth be told, for a good deal else besides, but which, being a religious boy, I wasn't supposed to think about.

Northern writers like to have it both ways. They set their achievements against the sometimes imaginary squalor of their origins and gain points for transcendence while at the same time implying that northern life is richer and in some undefined way truer and more honest than a life of southern comfort. 'Look, we have come through' is the stock version of it, though why a childhood in the (ex-) industrial North should be thought a handicap as distinct from some featureless suburb in South London isn't plain. True, if you're born in Barnsley and set your sights on being Virginia Woolf, it isn't going to be roses all the way. And had she been born in Doncaster I can't imagine Ivy Compton-Burnett coming to much. Though she could have written *A Pit and its Pitfalls*.

Still, education was movement; it was departure. Towering above the mean streets from which many of their pupils came, the schools of Leeds were like liners, their rows of windows lit up on winter afternoons as if great ships of learning, waiting to bear their passengers away from the dirt and fog of this smoking city to the promise of another life, or at least a more distant one. Because though that other life might only mean an office or the counter of a better class of shop, it was at least elsewhere, not Leeds. So, like the steam trains loading up in the city's City and Central Stations, these schools were conveyances. Education was a way out.

There was another way out. The Infirmary behind the Town Hall was a way out, too, with the first-class passengers berthed round the corner in the Brotherton Wing, and up Beckett Street a poorer ship, St James's, where everyone travelled steerage, though some got no further than the cemetery they could see from the windows. Ships of hope; ships of fear.

All of which is better put by Richard Hoggart, writing about his own education at Cockburn High School.

> Walking home at about 4.15 or so in the middle of winter when the street lights have already begun to come on I would look round as I finished crossing the clinkered 'Moor' and still see over the house-tops, half a mile away, the pale yellow glow of its classrooms and corridors and its cupolas standing up half silvery-grey in the near-darkness. It exercised as powerful a pull on my imagination as Oxford's dreaming spires on Matthew Arnold's or Christminster on Jude the Obscure's.
>
> (*A Local Habitation*, 1988)

The year I graduated at Oxford happened to be the year Richard Hoggart published *The Uses of Literacy*, which was both a celebration of and a lament for working-class culture. Since much of it was about Leeds, it rang all sorts of bells, but partly because Hoggart was writing about Hunslet and not Headingley and because I thought him closer to my parents' generation than my own, I saw his book as a description of their lives rather than mine. Hunslet was nearer both topographically and socially to the mean streets of my grandmother's Wortley than it was to the more salubrious suburb of Armley where I'd been brought up. So, not for the first time – and it's a recurring theme in *Cocktail Sticks* – I felt our family wasn't typical; we no more made the lower grade than we did a higher one.

It was a time when much was being made in fiction and social commentary of the gulf that higher education opened up between working-class parents and their studious offspring. It was one of Dennis Potter's early themes and is the central concern of Brian Jackson and Dennis Marsden's *Education and the Working Class*, a book, judging from my pencilled notes on the end papers, that I seem to have studied quite carefully when I was in New York with *Beyond the Fringe* in 1962, partly, I suppose, because it was also a breath of home.

There seemed to be agreement that a working-class child educated at university found it difficult thereafter to come to terms with – relate to if you like (which I didn't much) – his or her parents who looked on bewildered at this graduate cuckoo they had reared in their back-to-back nest. I never found this the case . . . or my case anyway.

University was my sphere, home was theirs, and far from wanting my parents to adapt their way of going on to my 'university outlook' (whatever that was), what I wanted, once I'd stopped being embarrassed by them, was that they should remain the same as they had always been, or as I imagined them to have been. That this was as false in its own way as wanting them to defer to my newly acquired sophistication I did not yet see. I just knew I wasn't like the characters I read about in novels – *Sons and Lovers* I suppose a classic example – or some of the disillusioned graduates in Jackson and Marsden.

Once upon a time, as I say in the play, I had longed for my parents to be socially accomplished and anonymously middle class, unfazed by the occasional glass of sherry or, when coming to Oxford, going out to supper at the Randolph as other parents did. University – and more significantly show business – meant that I had changed tack and, being more socially at ease myself, what I was requiring of them now was that in a parody of conservation they should preserve their old-fashioned down-to-earth character as I recalled (and sometimes imagined) it from when I was a child.

Thus my letters home from Oxford and later from New York were written in a self-consciously homely tone which revived the extremes of dialect and 'Leeds talk' long after my parents had begun to discard them themselves. It's true that Dad for instance used to refer to the August Bank Holiday as 'Banky' as in 'Where are we off for Banky?' but that had been in the forties and casual conversation. To find the phrase resurrected and set down in one of my letters in the sixties together with other similar outmoded expressions seems self-conscious and condescending. To read my letters home now is shaming. What can they have thought? I had been seven years at Oxford and was now appearing on Broadway, and yet I still affected to address them as if we were all in a dialect farce.

It must have been around this time, too, that I stopped bothering about my northern accent. I never had much, though I'd made some attempt at Oxford to iron out its worst excesses, with vowels always the problem, though whether one said 'bath' or 'bath' of less moment (and less of a giveaway) than if you came out with 'batcher' instead of 'butcher'.

But of course accents didn't matter any more – not because the class structure had altered; it hadn't particularly – it was thanks, in large measure, to the Beatles. By the mid-sixties a provincial accent (with the possible exception of Wolverhampton) had become not unfashionable, an attribute one need not strive to get rid of or even tone down. Sexual intercourse may have begun in 1963 but so did freedom of speech.

By this time I was performing on the stage in *Beyond the Fringe* and beginning to write, though I detect there a progression in my writing voice corresponding to that of my speaking one. My first play *Forty Years On* (1968) was entirely metropolitan and not written, any bit of it, in the voice with which I'd been born and brought up, but in the one which I had (if a little patchily) acquired. Set in a public school, the play provided a potted cultural history of England from 1900 to 1940, seen through the eyes of an upper-class couple in an air-raid shelter in Claridge's, a far cry from the streets of Upper Armley where I'd spent the war and even further from the streets of Tong Road. My second play, *Getting On*, was metropolitan too, though less lofty, and it was not until 1971, ten years after I'd first gone on the stage, that with my first TV film *A Day Out* I began to write plays in the voice with which I'd been born.

That I should have ended up in the theatre hardly seemed to surprise my parents. 'Folks did clap,' Mam said, after they had seen the opening performance of *Beyond the Fringe* in Edinburgh in August 1960, but there was no surprise in the remark, theatre, like university, another sphere in which they could not nor wanted to follow me. It had never been one of my own ambitions, though I'd been going to the theatre since I was a small child, taken there first by my grandmother who every year would give us an outing to the pantomime at the Theatre Royal in Lands Lane. It was never the Grand or the Empire, still less the much more disreputable City Varieties. It was always the blue and gold Theatre Royal where, long after Christmas, and even in May, the panto would still be running and we would toil up the scrubbed wooden stairs and come out on what at first seemed the almost sheer face of the gallery.

Invariably produced by Francis Laidler, it seemed a spectacular show and would, I think, seem so even today with transformation scenes, a flying ballet and a troupe of Tiller Girls. The star of the show would be a famous name from the music hall – Norman Evans, Frank Randle or Albert Modley – and these were always the bits Grandma enjoyed best.

These early visits to the pantomime stopped with the death of Grandma and the demolition of the Theatre Royal which came not long afterwards. My theatregoing then was confined to Saturday afternoons and the matinees at the Grand, nowadays the home of Opera North. By

London standards it was a huge theatre and, sitting in the gods and already short-sighted but still without glasses, I could never see the actors' faces (nor even knew that one was meant to). And they were distinguished actors too, as in those days shows toured before and after they went into the West End still with their original cast. So I saw Edith Evans in James Bridie's *Daphne Laureola*, Flora Robson playing a troubled shoplifter in *Black Chiffon*, Eric Portman as a Labour colonial governor in *His Excellency* and dozens of plays where the furnishings were by the Old Times Furnishing Company and the cigarettes were by Abdulla and nylons by Kayser-Bondor.

Cracks began to appear in this safe little world when later in the fifties I saw *Waiting for Godot* here, Olivier in *The Entertainer* and Dennis Lotis in the pre-London try-out of Osborne's *The World of Paul Slickey*. Even Olivier didn't draw the crowds, the theatre virtually empty, but so the theatre always was on a Saturday matinee and I took this as a matter of course, theatres like churches not meant to be full.

It was a shock when in 1951 I went to my first London theatre, the shortly to be demolished St James's. I could not get over how small it was. Laurence Olivier and Vivien Leigh were alternating *Antony and Cleopatra* and *Caesar and Cleopatra* and I saw the Shaw, remembering now only my wonder that, though I was in the cheapest seats, for the first time in my life I could see the faces of the actors.

There was no difficulty in that department the first time I appeared on the London stage, as it was in *Beyond the Fringe* at the Fortune, one of the smallest (as well as the steepest) of the London theatres and opposite the stage door of Drury Lane where *My Fair Lady* was still playing. We met everybody at that time and I wish I'd kept more of a diary, though it would just have been a list of celebrities who had come backstage and who I dutifully listed in my weekly letters home.

Harold Macmillan, the Prime Minister, came to be harangued by Peter Cook, imitating Harold Macmillan on the stage. In Washington we were taken along to the press conference when President Kennedy first revealed the existence of the Cuban missiles. My chief recollection of which is how briskly Kennedy strode to the podium and got on with the proceedings and how he flirted with and charmed the older women journalists.

The Cuban crisis was brewing all the time we were on tour with the revue, and the night it opened on Broadway was the night the Soviet ships were intercepted and turned back. At one point during the first night a siren sounded and the audience went utterly silent, only for it to turn out to be just a police siren. And I remember lying awake at night listening for the sound of breaking glass, because it was thought if war were going to come the first signs of it would be looting and rioting in the streets.

In due course after the crisis, the Kennedys themselves came to the show, the red telephone was installed in the box office and backstage thronged with Secret Servicemen, who, ironically in view of what was to happen the following year, were deeply suspicious of the wooden rifle we used in one of our sketches. The Kennedys came backstage, as did Adlai Stevenson along with fabled stars of the movies, but I've no memories of anything that was said. Like so many occasions in one's life, including some of its most intimate moments, one would like to have been there without being actually present, a fly, as it were on one's own wall, just watching.

So much of *Cocktail Sticks* is to do with class, it's appropriate I should end fairly high up the social scale in Downing Street. Several years after *Beyond the Fringe*, when Harold Wilson was Prime Minister, I was invited to a dinner at Downing Street for Prime Minister Trudeau. It was during the period when Harold Wilson imagined himself an English Kennedy, and when figures from the world of show-business and entertainment began to be allowed in at the front door.

My welcome wasn't all that auspicious. Mr and Mrs Wilson were lined up with Prime Minister Trudeau at the top of the stairs, and when Trudeau asked me what I did, I said I was a playwright, but had started off as an actor, in revue. Mary Wilson frowned. 'I hope it wasn't one of those revues where there is no scenery and they just wear black sweaters and so on.' I had to admit that it was, in fact, *Beyond the Fringe*. Now it was Mr Wilson's turn to frown. He looked at me suspiciously. '*Beyond the Fringe*? But you weren't one of the original four.' I said, 'Yes.' 'Well, I don't remember you. Are you sure?' So, feeling like Trotsky must have felt when he was cut out of the history of the Revolution, I then went into dinner, where the guest opposite, a noted London publisher, had the seating altered so that he could be opposite someone of more importance, and at a later stage in the meal one of the legs of my chair came off.

Alan Bennett, October 2012

.

Cocktail Sticks was first performed in the Lyttelton auditorium of the National Theatre, London, on 5 December 2012.

Alan Bennett Alex Jennings
Mam Janet Dale
Dad Jeff Rawle

with Derek Hutchinson and Maggie McCarthy

Director Nicholas Hytner
Designer Bob Crowley
Lighting Designer Tom Snell
Music George Fenton
Sound Designer John Leonard

AB I came home yesterday to sort through some things.

Neighbour 1 How's your mam?

AB Nicely. Only her memory's gone.

Neighbour 1 That can be a blessing. Where is she now?

AB Weston-super-Mare. Near my brother.
I don't say she's in a home.

Neighbour 1 She'll be in a home only he didn't say.

Neighbour 2 In Weston-super-Mare?

Neighbour 1 Near his brother, apparently.

Neighbour 2 Not near anywhere else.

AB The place was so cold. I thought I'd make a start on the kitchen cupboard. It's a green and cream plastic job Dad fixed on the wall above the draining board with a sliding door that always sticks.

Sound of door sticking.

There are tins of stuff here so antiquated they could figure on stalls at car boot sales specialising in kitchen collectables, and if I were a proper writer I'd make a list of all these for future reference.

An ounce or so of flour in a crumpled Be-Ro bag; some ancient Oxo, remains of my mother's little solitary meals. And as I embark on what is in effect a labour of culinary archaeology, turning out the rusting tins of ground nutmeg, the bottle of Goodall's Vanilla Essence, the two ancient glacé cherries nestling in an eggcup and a blackened bottle of cochineal I remember how well and how indistinguishably both she and my father had baked. Here is a tin of ground white pepper and with no such thing as a pepper mill in the house I wonder how we could ever have hoped to understand one another when we even use different kinds of pepper. I sweep out the rubble of spilled flour, stray currants and sugar, and sponge away at the hardened drizzle of some Worcester sauce. Then, right at the back, pushed into a far corner behind a dog-eared packet of desiccated coconut, I come across a little cylinder in clear plastic that is still clean and quite new.

It is a tube of cocktail sticks.

Sound of typing, of paper being unrolled from a typewriter which AB, aged forty, reads.

'There are fashions in childhood as in everything else.
The taste in idylls alters.
A boy in short trousers wanders across a broad country landing and from the shelves of sun-bleached classics (the wasps dying in the window) takes down a book.
But he is not me.'

Mam (*calling from another room*) Alan.

AB 'He lies flat on his stomach on the matchless lawn lapping up *Biggles* or *Swallows and Amazons*. His head is propped on his hands and his knees are bent after the manner of a boy reading in illustrations by E. H. Shepard.
But he is not me.'

Mam (*still in another room*) Alan. There's some tea.

AB 'Or, did one want to take it further back, that prep school on the south coast where on misty autumn afternoons one can hear the guns in Flanders, fall in love with a future Cabinet minister and make friends among one's contemporaries with boys destined to be of great eminence in the arts – a poet, a photographer, a man of letters. And all somehow a generation.'

The door opens.

Mam Can I fetch my tea in there?
I won't talk.

Mam comes in and sits on a hard chair by the door. Pause.

Are you doing your swotting?

AB Though I had written half-a-dozen plays by this time, three of them for the West End, my work for my mother remained what it had been twenty-five years before when I was sixteen and going in for my Higher School Certificate, an activity that was mysterious and out of reach:
'Your swotting.'
'Mam,' I said. 'Why did I have no childhood?'

Mam No childhood?
We took you to Morecambe.
We went to the panto.
You played with your pals.
You even had roller skates at one point.
Only it would be with us not being well off.
Do you need both bars on?
I'd be stifled in here.

Sound of electric fire being turned off.

AB What about the thirties? Were you aware of the storm clouds gathering?

Mam Well, we hadn't been married long.

AB And there was the Spanish Civil War.

Mam We always got the *Yorkshire Evening Post*. It might not have been in there.

I don't know why you wanted this shade of green. I wouldn't do a toilet in this colour.

I remember Korea because you nearly had to go.

AB I remember that. I was eighteen. It's childhood I'm talking about. Why did I have no childhood?

Mam Well, you never went short.

AB Exactly. And the upshot is I land up as an adult person without any baggage. Childhood's supposed to last you through life, a proper childhood. It's your sandwiches if you're a writer, your packed lunch. And because I never went short when I was little, now I'm starving.

Northern Voice Class, that's what you're on about.

AB This was J. B. Priestley, whom I met once.

Priestley You should be proud of your heritage.

AB It wasn't a heritage, it was an absence of heritage. Virginia Woolf never played out.

Priestley You didn't see Proust on roller skates.

AB This is what I'm complaining about – the non-presence of E. M. Forster in the Tower Ballroom, Blackpool.

Priestley Class, that's what you mean.

AB Dingy, threadbare, ordinary – it's not the stuff of literature.

Priestley Anything can be the stuff of literature. *Nothing* can be the stuff of literature. Look at bloody Samuel Beckett.

Mam Would it be the war?

Dad It was never the war. Childhoods don't stop because of the war. It wasn't like bananas. They didn't shut down for the duration. They happen, childhoods. They occur. You have them willy-nilly.

You should have had the childhood I had. I was glad to see the back of mine.

AB This is my father, who had died a few years previously. He is standing outside the ladies' lavatory in Schofield's department store, holding a handbag. The handbag belongs to my mother.

Mam I don't like to take it in with me in case I have to put it on the floor.

Dad In which case it would be polluted until the end of time. It's a wonder I've escaped arrest for as long as I have. I've waited with her flaming handbag outside every toilet in the West Riding.

And it gets more and more prolonged.

Once upon a time, she would have been in and out, only nowadays she seems to have to have an all-over wash afterwards.

AB To signal that the handbag is not his, Dad holds it slightly apart from himself as if it is in some sense distasteful. And yet, as I will one day come to see, this was a kind of declaration too, and the holding of his wife's handbag one of the 'austere and lonely offices' of love.

Dad Of course you had a childhood and we've got the snaps to prove it.

AB Why were we so ordinary?

Dad Everybody was ordinary then. You were ordinary when you lived round us.

AB Why have I got no memories?

Dad Because we were happy, that's why. And Alan –

AB What?

Dad Look after your mam.

Mam Here's the toilet.
  Take my handbag.

AB Mam. I won't.

Mam You can put it under your raincoat.

AB No.

Mam I do miss your dad.

AB Cheated of childhood though I feel in middle age, this is nothing new as I was already feeling the same at the time.

Interviewer We are in your first school which was . . .

AB Upper Armley National School.
  That's right, the walls hung with oilcloth charts of birds and the wonders of the natural world. The treasures of the seashore.
  And I knew they were a con.

Interviewer A con? You were eight.

AB All the birds you ever saw in Leeds were brown. The shore at Morecambe, which according to the chart was alive with crabs and sea horses and studded with starfish – that was brown too.

Interviewer Not everywhere was like that.

AB Leeds was.
  Morecambe was.
  Even language was.
  Did you ever come across sward?

Interviewer Sward?

AB It's what they call grass in stories. Lush, thick grass you have picnics on or knights gallop over. I asked the teacher if there was sward in Leeds and if that was sward on the rec in Moorfield Road. She said it was.

Dog dirt and thin grass, it was never sward. Leeds didn't run to sward or Morecambe to starfish.

At the age of eight I knew that books were a con.

Interviewer What's your next record?

AB I can see now, could see then probably, that the childhood I hankered for was drawn from my reading of memoirs of the twenties and was well out of fashion by the 1960s when poor or deprived childhoods were becoming the thing. Except that mine didn't qualify on that score either, deprived only in that it was short on deprivation and light on despair.

A few years after Dad died I am ordering some coal in Yorkshire.

'Mr Redhead? It's Alan Bennett.'

Mr Redhead Oh my goodness. I am conversing with higher beings.

AB Can I have some coal?

Mr Redhead You can. Though I have to say, however celebrated you are you'll never be a patch on your dad.

AB That was how my father was always remembered – his face brimming with goodwill, and Mam too. A lovely couple. Except if you're their son and want drama, deprivation or even disappointment.

Eventually I would come to see that the meagreness of my childhood and my sparse memories of it could be a subject in itself. But this realisation took time and I was still complaining about it to my mother in 1976 when I was already in my forties.

Literature, you see, one needs credentials.

Mam You've been to college. You've got your cap and gown, what more credentials do you want?

AB I want a past that's a bit larger than life. I wish I'd had a harder time.

Mam We do our best, let you stay on at school and go away to college and now you're saying you wish we'd sent you out to work at sixteen. You might have been like Eric Portman. He had to work as an assistant in a gents' outfitters in Halifax. I've been in the shop many a time. He was sensitive, you could tell that.

AB Do you mean he was homosexual?

Mam I mean he was polite to his mother and didn't come out with words like that.

AB Actually that last bit I didn't say and nor did she, but that was what you did with dialogue when you were a writer, edited and augmented it for public consumption. It wasn't lying; it was part of the job. The truth was I didn't have any unfortunate sexual experiences.

Mam Yes, you did. There was that feller at the pictures. I'll never forgive myself for that.

AB The film was *The Sea Hawk* with Errol Flynn.

Mam It's not a U. It's an A. And I'm not going, I've seen it.

AB I'll ask somebody to take me in.

Mam Make sure it's a woman. Don't ask a man.

AB I didn't ask a man. A man asked me. He may even have paid for my ticket.

Mam What do you mean, he felt your legs?

AB He felt my legs. Said they were nice. He said they were fat. Are they fat?

Whenever we went out as children Mam would say in a ritual that seemed to persist until the eve of my call-up, 'Don't stop with any strange men.' And that afternoon at the pictures I realised this was one of them.

My father now comes home from work.

Mam Our Alan's been assaulted.

Dad Where?

Mam The Picturedrome.

Dad Are you sure he's not making it up? He's always coming home telling the tale.

AB I'm not. He put his hand on my leg.

Mam On it or up it?

Dad (*embarrassed*) Mam.

AB Dad was embarrassed.

You didn't believe me, Dad. I was sexually interfered with at the age of ten and you didn't want to know.

Dad I was embarrassed. I'm embarrassed now.

AB You can't be embarrassed, Dad. You're dead. (And you didn't die of embarrassment.)

Dad Your memory of me's embarrassed, that's what it is. Anyway you weren't interfered with. He put his hand on your leg.

Mam That's foreplay.

Dad It never is. It's before foreplay is that. It's not even the run-up to foreplay. Not that foreplay is ever a word I would have used.

And what about women? They have to cope with that practically every day of their lives. It's an occupational hazard of being a woman, a hand on your leg.

AB Not these days.

Dad How? Are men different now?

AB No. Women are.

The cinema manager had a thin moustache and wore a dinner jacket. He was the most sophisticated man I'd ever seen.

Mam A gentleman put his hand on my little boy's leg during the matinee.

AB It was nothing, Mam.

Cinema Manager Did he do anything else?

AB No.

Mam But he could have done. There's no telling what it might have led to.

AB What it actually led to was two free seats for the first house on Saturday night, given to Mam out of sheer embarrassment. I was embarrassed. Dad was embarrassed. The cinema manager was embarrassed. Embarrassment, I began to see, ruled the world. And for that at least I had my childhood to thank.

The damage, if damage there was, had nothing to do with my leg and the hand on it or up it. What remains in the memory was my father's refusal to believe me. When I began to regret the absence of a childhood I could at least console myself with that: I had been damaged and that was satisfying. Still, it didn't amount to what they nowadays call trauma. Philip Larkin says they fuck you up, your mum and dad. And if you end up writing that's fine, because if they have fucked you up then you've got something to write about. But if they haven't fucked you up you don't have anything to write about so then they've fucked you up good and proper.

When I complained to Mam that my life did not measure up to the lives I read about in books, it ought to have been familiar ground to my mother, who often grumbled at just that herself. Her regular reading was the *Woman's Own* with its resident columnists Monica Dickens and Beverley Nichols. The more glamorous magazines like *Ideal Home* she would read at Miss Pemberton's the hairdresser's and it was from such publications that Mam constructed her vision of how most people lived – apart, that is, from us.

Mam Alan. What are cocktáils?

AB It's cócktails.

Mam Cocktáils.

AB No. Cócktails. The emphasis isn't on the tails . . . it's on . . . the other.

Mam Anyway, what are they?

AB Martinis. Gin and tonic. Whisky and soda. All sorts.

Mam They have a cherry in them.

AB Some of them do. It depends.

Mam But they're proper drinks. They couldn't be Ribena?

AB No. Why?

Mam I keep reading about these cocktail parties in *Woman's Own*. Stuff on sticks. Folks standing round conversing, little sandwiches you can make with the crusts cut off. I wish we could do with alcohol. Folks that like a drink are lucky because that introduces you to people. Say 'I'll have a small sherry' and it oils the wheels. Whereas if you say 'Mr Bennett has to watch his stomach' it puts a damper on the proceedings straight away.

The other thing they have are these coffee mornings.

AB Yes.

Mam Which is a beggar because we aren't keen on coffee either. Oh, and you know I was asking you about these chaise longues? I saw a picture of one the other day. It's only a settee with the end cut off.

I think there's a lot of that.

AB What?

Mam Calling stuff by fancy names when there's no need. It makes you feel shut out.

Dad What would you talk about at these coffee mornings?

Mam Current affairs. Fashion. General topics.

Dad What do you know about current affairs?

Mam Our Alan can tell me.

Beverley Nichols has cats. He talks about them. We've got a cat.

Dad We've also got mice. You could talk about them.

Mam You stunt me, you. You won't even try and be sophisticated.

Dad Well, you should have married him.

Mam Who?

Dad Beverley Nichols.

Mam I shouldn't think he's the marrying sort.

Peals of laughter.

AB Dad had no social aspirations at all and got all he wanted of company serving in the shop. They would go to the pictures once or twice a week and on Sundays to high tea at Grandma's and on Wednesday afternoons they'd have a little bus ride to Otley or Ilkley and he seemed to ask no more of life.

She did, though, feeling much more than him that self-sufficiency amounted to eccentricity. And worse.

Cut to twenty years later.

Dad Mam. The doctor's going to ask you one or two questions.

Mam What is it I've done?

Doctor You haven't done anything, Mrs Bennett. You're not well.

AB My mother was haunted all her life by the fear of TB. No matter that antibiotics had effectively eradicated TB well within her lifetime, the fear of it remained. What neither she nor my father ever expected to have to cope with was mental illness. That was for what my mother called 'the better class', so that when she was suddenly struck down with depression it seemed an affliction to which she was not socially entitled. She and my father were so diffident and unassuming they didn't feel they even merited despair, with neurosis as much a social distinction as an affliction.

Mam I've let everybody down.

Dad Nay, you never have.

Mam I have. You don't know. Look at the house, it's filthy.

Dad It never is.

Doctor Mr Bennett, please.

Mam Folks know.

Doctor What do they know?

Mam Everybody else is the same. Having folks round. We're not. We're not the same.

Doctor How? How are you not the same?

Mam Everybody else sits down to a proper breakfast. We never do.

Doctor Mrs Bennett. Nobody's going to blame you for that.

Mam That's just the start. We're not the same.

AB So laugh though Mam and Dad did years before, Mam's enquiries about cocktail parties weren't an attempt to go up the social ladder, but just one more example of how we as a family were in dereliction of our duties.

Dad Who could we ask? We know nobody – or nobody who'd want anything besides a cup of tea.

Mam That's what I'm saying. We never have people round.

Dad We have your Kathleen round. She's never away.

Mam I mean to a meal.
  The pinnacle of my social life is a scrutty bit of lettuce and tomato and some tinned salmon.
  Mind you, I read in *Ideal Home* that if you mix tinned salmon with this soft cheese you can make it into one of these moussy things. Shove a bit of lemon on it and it looks really classy.
  Another thing is, if you can put your hands on the right ingredients, olive oil, for instance, you can make your own salad dressing. They do it all the time abroad apparently. Well, you can get olive oil at Timothy White's. We might still have some. I got it to soften the wax in my ears.

AB This would be in the early fifties, when the writings of Elizabeth David had not yet blazed a trail to Leeds. But there was a more crucial objection to even the humblest of social gatherings to do with living over the shop.

Mam Dad. Do you have to make your own dripping?

Dad Why?

Mam The stink. How can I have a cocktail party upstairs when you're rendering dripping in the cellar?

AB In this she was right, as twice a week at least the house would reek with the stench of melting fat. It was why she didn't like anybody to call and why 'your pals', as my mother called them, were seldom invited either.

Dad Don't write that down, Doctor. It was only fat. I was a butcher after all.

AB Once when we were little my brother told me he had woken up to hear our parents fighting in the middle of the night, something neither of us could credit. Now, years later I wake and hear them laughing and talking with seemingly no thought that it's three in the morning.

That there may have been a less innocent side to these cheerful chats would have been unthinkable to me at the time.

Dad Why?

AB You were my parents. I didn't like to associate you with the sexual act. Besides, I was seventeen and deeply religious.

Dad Maybe that was one of the things we talked about.

Mam I like him going to church, only I don't want him becoming a vicar.

Dad Well, he looks the part.

Mam Dad.

Laughter.

Dad He'll have to put it on a bit more. He's too Leeds for a proper parson.

Mam Well, now he's going to college he may come back with more of an educated twang.

Dad We'll have to mind our 'p's and 'q's.

Mam What for?

Dad If we're a parson's parents.
  I hope it won't mean functions. We don't want roping in for any of that.

Mam Well, I expect vicars have cocktails same as any anyone else.

Dad Maybe he'll change his ideas when he gets to college. The way students go on, God is generally the first casualty.

Mam Why does he want to be a vicar, though?

Dad It's what the mirror tells him he's suited for – vicar, librarian, teacher. I never wanted to be a butcher.

Mam Yes, but you were beautiful.

  They laugh again.

Stop it, Dad. He'll think there's something going on.

Dad Well, he's not a vicar yet.

  More laughter.

AB And just as it never occurs to me that there might be a post-coital element to this talk and laughter, that there might be a related element to my nightly patrols of the streets of North Leeds never occurs to them either.

Mam Our Alan? No. He's shy.

AB As indeed I was.

  Footsteps.

Man Have you got a light?

AB Sorry, I don't smoke. (*Pause.*) But thank you all the same.
  It is not generally known – or is known only to the devout (which at the age of seventeen includes me) that

confession isn't just for Catholics and that the Church of England too makes provision for oral and individual confession.

And whereas the Catholics get away with easy generalities, Anglicans are expected to be specific, which is embarrassing enough – and worse, whereas the RCs get a box to hide their shame Anglicans have to kneel next to the actual priest as I am now doing.

Vicar How long is it since your last confession, my child?

AB I think it's about six months – no, four months – or maybe a bit longer . . . possibly . . .

Vicar It's not important. What sins have you committed?

AB I begin, of course with the sin of sins, or 'tossing off' as I would call it were I not in church.

Vicar Abuse of your God-given body.

AB I'm not sure he doesn't stifle a yawn. He is bored, having rightly divined that this shy, spectacled boy is plainly not one of the great wankers of the world. DNA is as yet undiscovered and would in any case have to have achieved some degree of sophistication to register the infinitesimal quantities of semen I had produced. So we pass on.

Vicar Anything else, my child?

AB Embarrassment at being called my child is probably a sin too, but I let it lie, reminding me as it does of something else. 'My parents embarrass me.' The vicar perks up. This is odd. It is not usual.

Vicar Indeed? What do they do to embarrass you, my child?

AB They don't do anything really.

How explain that, apart from being themselves, it's because, living over the shop, they've managed to acquire accommodation where the front door opens straight off the alley into the living room, or that on one of the few occasions one of my few indubitably middle-class friends comes round my father puts a pan on the dining table.

The Vicar waits.

They just do.

Vicar It will pass, my child.

AB Loosed from my burden of sin, I skip out into the streets of Headingley. Though not for long.

At the end of school and, as I see it, the beginning of life is a black, greasy unfordable sump – National Service – a commandeering of one's life which takes me first to Pontefract and the depot of the York and Lancaster Regiment for basic training.

Band music.

Dad Why are you roaring? He's finished the worst part and he's right enough. Here he comes.

Mam (*crying*) I saw our Clarence pass out before he went to the front.

Dad There isn't a front.

Mam There is. There's Korea.

AB Mam, I'm not going to Korea. I've told you. I'm going on the Russian course. It's a real cushy number. You wear your own clothes. You go to Cambridge.

That I survived that first six weeks surprises me even today, the rest of my squad steelworkers from Sheffield who, after the parade, adjourn with their parents to the nearest pub. We, typically, find somewhere that bit more refined: a little hotel at Ackworth, an eighteenth-century enclave amid the all encompassing coalfields. After six weeks of being harried from dawn to dusk the comfort and the peace of it is hard to believe, with Mam more cheerful and Dad more loving than I have ever seen them.

And I was never so far from shame about my parents than at that passing-out parade at Pontefract when we were, however briefly, just like everybody else.

Mam You're hungry.

Look, Dad, he's polished off all the scones and mine as well. We've fetched you a cake.

AB Twenty years down the road and two days after Dad's death I remembered that afternoon. It was the first time I ever really thought he loved me.

Mam In bed the night you were called up he cried.

AB Over-mothered, under-fathered, I found this a surprise. Why did you weep, Dad? I'd never seen you weep ever.

Dad Shut up about it.

AB Dad. You're dead. We can talk about it now.

Dad You were that young.

AB I was eighteen.

Dad You were a boy still. You didn't even shave. I was bothered what might happen to you.

AB Being killed?

Dad Before that. The other lads.

AB They swore – which you never did – but they were right enough.

Dad I never went. In 1939.

Mam You couldn't go. You were in a reserved occupation.

AB That was true.

With butchering a reserved occupation, Dad was not called up. The battlefield butchering would be done by the conscripts, the amateurs, while the professional butchers stayed at home.

Dad I didn't want to join up.

AB This was true – but he didn't want to join up because joining up would have meant joining in – and our family was never any good at that.

Mam Mixing. We can't mix.

AB This was true and war made no difference – unblitzed, unevacuated, unenlisted, my father's civilian status a casualty of my family's failure ever to be in the swim. And war made no difference. History was not for us.

Seldom even recognising there was an occasion to be risen to, we had missed Mr Chamberlain's momentous broadcast on the declaration of war.

Mam Well, we were on a tram. We were at Whingate going down into Leeds.

AB To dip out of the national mood was my parents' instinctive reaction in 1939 as it still is mine.

And as at the beginning of the war so at the end: it would have taken more than the cessation of hostilities in Europe to get my parents doing the hokey-cokey.

Dad Splother, that's all it is.

AB We never even went to a street party. So self-stigmatised though they were and seldom in step, this didn't mean my parents were out of step as people; they just weren't part of the parade.

Dad When our Gordon was born and I found myself a father I walked halfway across Leeds to tell my brothers –

your uncles – about this addition to the family. That wasn't splother.

AB And as with birth so with its opposite, and when death came to my father it had this to be said for it, that this was one of the rare occasions when he found himself doing the same as everyone else. Death, like his late passing of the driving test, meant for my father that he had joined the human race – if only on the point of leaving it.

Still, in 1952 death for my father was twenty years down the road and that afternoon at Pontefract when as right marker for Ladysmith squad I marched past, my parents and I were united in happiness and relief. They were proud of me. I was not ashamed of them; they were, however briefly, normal people.

Of course it didn't last.

The shaming truth was that for most of my childhood the parents I want are a dull middle-class couple, the man a solicitor perhaps or even a bank manager, his wife, my mother, a neat capable soft-tweeded lady whom life could not ambush or surprise, a couple who could negotiate with ease – an ease, I may say, I notably lacked myself – any social situation with aplomb.

Dad With what?

AB Aplomb. Confidence. Self-possession.

Dad Right.

AB I knew, of course, that Mam in particular would want to come and see me at Oxford as she had looked at pictures of the city and its architecture and scarcely believed I could inhabit such an enchanting place.

Mam Is it like school?

AB You go to lectures and once or twice a week you write an essay for your tutor.

Mam Have you been getting good marks?

AB They don't do it like that.

Mam That's a shame. You always got such good marks when you were a kiddy. You jumped a class twice and you were always the youngest in the class. Is it a big class?

AB It's not a class. They teach you individually or sometimes two at a time.

Mam Just you and him?

AB Yes.

Mam Is that because you're one of the cleverest?

AB No. And I'm not anyway.

Mam You always say that. Isn't it a bit embarrassing, just you and him?

AB Yes. It's a bit like going to see the doctor every week.
As time went on the questioning got more specific.

Mam Have you seen Balliol College?

AB It's pronounced Bay-liol. Why?

Mam Beverley Nichols went there. He sometimes writes about it in the *Woman's Own*. Why didn't you go there?

AB Because it's a smart college and everybody who goes there has to be clever.
Besides I wouldn't have wanted to. It's ugly and Victorian. It looks like St James's Hospital.

Mam Beverley Nichols was President of the Union. I was a bit surprised.

AB Why?

Mam I shouldn't have thought he was Labour.

AB It's not that kind of union.

Mam He had lots of cocktail parties, apparently. You haven't had any.

AB Not to date, no.
The Rector had a sherry party. I went to that. Everybody went to that.

Mam Is it picturesque?

AB What?

Mam Exeter College.

AB A bit. What do you think?

Mam I wouldn't know. We've not been asked.

AB I sent you a postcard.
Eventually it could be put off no longer.

Mam When your dad and me come down to see you, you've no need to go round with us. You'll have your studying to do.

AB Well, we'll see.

Mam We can go round by ourselves then just have tea and a toasted teacake with you somewhere. We won't show you up.

Dad Why do they call them dons?

AB I had to confess I didn't know, though the word had a Spanish flavour and before I came up I had vaguely associated it with that cloaked and mysterious hidalgo that used to advertise Sandeman's Port.

Mam They all look very refined. More than they do at the university in Leeds. I see some of the lecturers waiting at the tram stop and they look right ordinary. Even the feller on the gate seems a cut above the rest.

AB He's just the porter.

Mam He's very polite. Called you Mr Bennett.

Dad You mustn't have your aunties coming down.

AB God forbid.

Dad They're busting to come. I should think everybody who's been into Manfield's in the last six months has been regaled with the 'My nephew's at Oxford' saga.

AB On the few occasions my parents did come to Oxford I smuggled them in and out of college as quickly as I could and almost put a sack over their unoffending heads. The shame of those times – and the shame now for the shame then – is vivid still, more vivid for me, I hope, than it ever was for them.

I wished I could take a leaf out of Russell Harty's book. He was on the same staircase as I was and he hadn't been there long before his parents, Fred and Myrtle, came down from Blackburn to see how 'our Russell' was doing, their arrival signalled by a white Jaguar, the emblem of successful greengrocery, parked outside the college lodge.

Fred, plump and bottle-nosed, dressed in loud tweeds, Myrtle a little bird of a woman, highly painted and teetering along on high heels and leopardskin coat. They had money and they didn't mind showing it and they were undeniably common. By comparison my parents were Harold Nicolson and Vita Sackville-West.

Russell was entirely unabashed by his parents and even – though I never told my mother this – held a cocktail party for them to which he invited his friends, his tutors and even the Rector of the college. And of course they were a great hit.

Fred So you teach our Russell then, Mr Coghill?

Nevill Coghill Yes. He comes to me for early Middle English. Chaucer and so on.

Fred And how's he doing?

Coghill Well, Russell has a lively mind and an inquiring one. I don't think, though, he's going to turn out an academic.

Fred An academic what?

Coghill A teacher.

Fred Well, he's not going to be a greengrocer.

Myrtle Mr Harty has a stall in Blackburn Market. It's at the better end. Fruit and vegetables. He's a bit of a pioneer in the field.

Fred I was instrumental in introducing Blackburn to the avocado pear.

Coghill Really? And did it take off?

Fred Among the more discerning of my customers, yes, Mr Coghill, it did.

Myrtle It's for salads and suchlike. It needs a spot of salad cream to liven it up and a prawn or two. I was initially opposed to it, wasn't I, Fred, but I've come round to it now. Repeats a bit, of course.

Fred The avocado was only the first step. Next on the list is the artichoke.

I gather they're a bugger to eat but quite tasty when you get to the heart. Do you just teach English? You don't take him for anything else?

Myrtle Our Russell says that he's a bit on the cheeky side.

Coghill He is indeed. That's exactly what he is, Mrs Harty. Cheeky. The cheek of Chaucer. Yes. Very good, very good . . .

Fades.

AB Artichokes were beginning to figure in Mam's hankerings too.

Mam I wish we went out a bit more.

Dad We do go out.
  We go a bus ride practically every week. Otley, Ilkley, Harrogate.

Mam I don't mean that.

Dad Well, what do you mean?

Mam I'd like to go to cafés now and again.

Dad We do go to cafés. We never go out but what we go to a café.

Mam No. I mean proper cafés – where the waiter's a man and they come with the pepper.
  A café where everything doesn't have tea, bread and butter included.
  I was reading about these artichokes.

Dad What about them?

Mam They'll sometimes kick off with them, apparently.

Dad Well, don't go and get yourself one.

Mam Why not?

Dad Because it'll be the avocado pear saga all over again.

Mam Well, how was I to know?
  I thought they were something you had to finish off with. Only it wasn't like a proper pear. Right sickly. And a shocking stone. You have them in cocktails now apparently.

Dad What?

Mam Avocados. With prawns.

Dad In a cocktail? How do you drink that?

Mam I don't know. It's another world.

AB Though I ended up staying at Oxford for eight years, what I actually did there was always a mystery to my parents. And when I abandoned academic life to appear in the revue *Beyond the Fringe* the mystery remained.

Mam What is it you're going to do on the stage? Is it like turns?

AB I suppose. They call it satire.

Dad It's not cheeky?

AB How do you mean?

Dad Smut.

AB Actually, no. It's remarkably free of smut, in fact.

Mam So who is it you're taking off?

AB Politicians. The Royal Family. The Church of England. I do a sermon.

Dad What's it going to be called, this show?

AB *Beyond the Fringe.*

Mam Is that because of your hair?

AB No.

Mam Do the others have fringes?

AB No.

Mam Well, I wish you didn't. It's always in your eyes. Most lads put their hair back when they're about fourteen only you somehow missed the moment. Still, it's a lovely colour. Can I cut a bit off and keep it in an envelope?

AB This was a regular ceremony with two or three of the resultant envelopes knocking about the sideboard drawer.

Periodically Mam would have a clear-out, compare the contemporary hair with that from 1947, say, and find the colour much the same.

Dad So wuther it. Dozy article, saving hair.

AB News of the triumph percolated through to my mother's sister, Aunty Kathleen. and became a perennial topic of conversation in Manfield's shoe shop on Commercial Street.

Aunty Kathleen Perhaps madam would like to try these. They are a seven but madam probably needs a broader fitting. I had a letter from my nephew this morning. Appearing in the West End.
    Rubbing shoulders with the stars apparently.
    I just want to make sure you've got plenty of room here –

Customer They feel quite comfy.

Aunty Kathleen Good. He was at Oxford originally but once he'd got his cap and gown he felt he had bigger fish to fry. I don't think you're ready for an eight. And they will stretch, of course. Would madam like some suede cleaner to accompany them?

AB After the West End came Broadway, from where I dutifully reported every week.

Mam Our Alan's met Charles Boyer.
    Oh, and Alexis Smith.

Dad Which is Alexis Smith?

Mam Tall classy woman. Hair swept up, a bit Joan Fontaine-ish. Used to play the secretary who married the boss.

Dad What does he find to say to them?

AB Not much was the truth of it. I just used to gape.

Mam Well, there's all sorts he can say. He can tell them how he saw them at the Picturedrome on Ridge Road during the war.

Dad That'll make him popular.

AB The pleasures of being so abruptly and unexpectedly propelled into theatrical success as we were in *Beyond the Fringe* and the acclaim on Broadway that followed was heightened because it brought with it no sense of entitlement. What after all entitled one to expect a knock on the dressing-room door and it's Bette Davis or to find oneself having supper with Christopher Isherwood?

That many of these fabled names were, to put it kindly, tinged with antiquity for me only glamourised them the more, with the wonder always bringing with it the question 'What am *I* doing here?'

A real (and lifelong) component of happiness, it seems to me, is never to lose this inner astonishment because, once lost, a lot of fun goes with it. Whether setting foot on a Broadway stage, having supper at the Savoy or, in my case, finding oneself in a strange bed, it's all much more fun if none of it seems quite one's due.

Mam Legends they were. We were queuing to see their films and now our Alan's rubbing shoulders with them.

Dad Where?

Mam A party apparently. Noël Coward was there too. And Adlai Stevenson.

Dad What was he in?

Mam I don't know. Wasn't he in westerns?

Dad Turn the wireless up. It's *Sunday Half Hour*.

A hymn, which Dad accompanies on his violin.

AB My father is a good violinist, largely self-taught and could pick up his fiddle and play along to the wireless and later the television, sometimes saying the notes as he plays them with what I take to be perfect pitch.

I thought this almost miraculous, but characteristically my father makes little of it himself as he does any of his accomplishments, the only achievement of which he is thoroughly proud still to come. This is after he has retired and they have moved from Leeds to a small village in the Dales, pastures new reviving Mam's thwarted social ambitions, now something of a joke. The business of retirement was not yet the industry it has since become and there were fewer guidelines.

Mam There's all sorts going on here. We're going to have to participate choose what your Dad says. We've started going to church again so at least we've put our toe in the water.

Dad If it was just church I wouldn't mind, only they follow up with a discussion over coffee. Well, we don't like coffee and besides it's about stuff we know nothing about. Last week it was the Third World. Well, your mam doesn't know where the Third World is.

Mam I do.

Dad Well, where is it then?

Mam It's somewhere beginning with A. I know. Abroad.

She bursts out laughing.

Dad This week it's Buddhism. Well, what does me and your mam know about Buddhism?

Mam He was fat. I know that.

And I know they're not supposed to cut their hair and they're nice to cows.

Dad It's Sikhs who don't cut their hair.

Mam Well, aren't Sikhs Buddhists? (*Calling.*) Alan.

AB They were having this conversation in bed.

Mam You've been to Oxford. Are Sikhs Buddhists?

AB I don't know.

Mam Well, you'd better come to church, then.

More laughter, fading.

AB Drink remained a problem because it was so mysterious.

Mam Well, your dad can't drink with his stomach and I don't like it. Even that bit they give you at Communion rifts up on me.

AB The effects of drink they hugely exaggerated.
The church was not far from the church [??] and they would walk there even in the worst possible weather. Mam would never let Dad drive to church lest the Eucharist should make him incapable on the return journey.

Mam Well, you laugh but they tell you not to drink and drive . . .

Fade.

AB Sherry was not entirely unknown in the house, a miniature bottle kept to add a tincture to the occasional trifle. The amount that was added was minute, almost homeopathic (the rifting-up factor again), the bottle lasting most of my childhood and well into adult life.

Mam We've bought a proper bottle of sherry now so we don't feel out of it. If folks don't want a cup of tea we're in a position now to offer them something stronger.

AB Which was true except, of course, that they were both of them unaware of the times when something stronger might be thought appropriate.

Thus the vicar, calling with the envelopes for the Free Will Offering scheme at ten o'clock in the morning was startled to be offered a bumper of sherry, so shocked that he accepted, with Mam just as anxious to help him to a top-up as she would have been were it tea.

Still, with sherry now on the agenda she felt they were en route at least to becoming a normal couple.

Nor did it stop there.

They rang me one night in London.

Mam Your dad and me have been down to the Brookses. And we've found an alcoholic drink we like.

AB What's that then?

Mam Dad. What was that alcoholic drink we had tonight?

Indistinguishable remark off.

Bitter lemon.

Well, love, the call's going on. We'll be writing to you tomorrow.

AB It pains me to say it but what transforms my parents' lives is not reading or an accession of sociability but my father's learning to drive. Coming at the age of sixty-five, this is a late turning point in his life, but still, passing the test made him feel that he is at last a member of the human race and that they have taken a large step towards being like other people.

So now, emancipated from the public transport they had depended on all their lives, every day they go off in their little khaki Mini – Kendal, Morecambe, Richmond, St Anne's – and with their flask and their sandwiches at last they see the world.

Mam I prefer the west end of Morecambe to the Battery end. It's more select.

Dad It's where we used to come during the war and you were roaring because I had to go back to Leeds.

Mam Well, there were bombs.

Dad Not properly. Why should they bomb Leeds? Rhubarb and ready-made suits – that wasn't going to impede the war effort.

Mam Alan's play's about the war, partly.

Dad Is it? I couldn't make it out.

Mam Well, they sang 'Run Rabbit Run'.

AB This was *Forty Years On*.

Dad It's a bit since we've seen him.

Mam It's with him acting in the play. Or else he's got a girl.

They laugh.

Dad Don't be daft. It's the car. He used to come up to give us a run round. Now I can drive he doesn't feel the need.

Mam He can't be ashamed of us any more else he wouldn't have introduced us to Sir John Gielgud. I said to him, 'Alan it was going to Oxford altered you. You stopped wearing a vest and started having your main meal at night.'

Dad He didn't want us eccentric when he was younger. He wanted us the same as everybody else. Now he doesn't seem to mind. Now it's you that wants us normal – folks coming in, entertaining.

Mam Now, Dad, don't start.

AB When Dad talked about Mam 'roaring' at Morecambe, which you generally do in the legitimate world with laughter, in Leeds meant to cry. 'Don't start roaring' a warning to a child to fetch it back from the brink of tears.

I roared a lot when I was a child – out of sheer rage or simply because I couldn't see another way out. Now I suppose the writing has replaced the roaring but the reasons are much the same.

Mam I just wish we could have gone abroad. When folks take out their snaps of the Costa Brava I'm always the odd one out.

Dad What would we do on the Costa Brava?

Mam What other folks do.

Dad Sunbathe and get tiddly? Don't be so daft. And I'll tell you something else about the Costa Brava: I bet it's barren of toasted teacakes.

AB Dad wasn't destined to enjoy their new-found mobility for long, dying of a heart attack when he was seventy-one. It was sudden and unexpected but could have been foreseen.

Mam had only just emerged from a bout of depression which had put her in the local hospital, though local actually meant thirty miles away. Her recurrent depressions, though they did not kill her, effectively killed him, as he had been driving to and from the hospital once and sometimes twice a day. Stunned by Dad's death it wasn't long before Mam had to be taken into hospital again. Meanwhile there was the funeral.

Sounds of a party.

Mam They're laughing and talking as if nothing has happened.

AB Well, it's the only time some of them see each other.

Mam What will they think next door?

AB Nothing, love.

Mam Have they got some tea? They'll want some sweet stuff.

AB That's all seen to.
'Was I there?' she asked a day or two later.
'Yes, only you were upset.'

Mam Well, he was a love was your Dad. We never had a wrong word. What was it he died of?

AB He had a heart attack.

Mam What would that be with?

AB Running backwards and forwards to the hospital to see you was the proper answer, but not one there was any point in giving. Cake.

Mam Cake?

AB He'd put on weight and what with driving and that he didn't take much exercise.

Mam He was grand. And lovely when he was young. Not a mark on him.

AB There had not been a mark on him at the hospital. Lying in Intensive Care after the heart attack they had attached electrodes to his chest, which, never having been exposed to the sun, was a creamy unblemished white, the skin above his collar and his face worn and red, the line between so sharp his head might have been a helmet.

Mam How long were we married?

AB Forty-six years.

Mam Well, we've done well.

AB Who?

Mam You and me.

AB Nay, Mam. It's me. I'm your son.

Sometimes she was better and almost happy, other times troubled and tearful and unable to locate in her mind or her memory the husband she had lost and who was still defined in terms of his fatherhood, 'Your dad' rather than being called by his name, Walter – a name nobody gets called today, though like Rowland it seems to me a grand and noble name.

It's understandable my father and I should often be conflated in my mother's mind as I was living at home and slipping with alarming ease into Dad's retirement routine of doing the shopping and much of the cooking and every afternoon taking Mam for a little run in the car.

It was unsurprising, too, that she should still occasionally try and enrol me in those social endeavours which Dad had always managed to quench or forestall.

With her memory patchy, the aspirations were faltering now, but were given new impetus because come the seventies the press and television began to preach the delights of retirement and the rolling back of old age.

Mam I'm starting going to classes.

AB What sort of classes?

Mam Pottery.

AB Didn't you go to painting classes?

Mam Did I?

Oh yes. They said it was for beginners, only when I got there I found they could all do it right well, it wasn't beginners at all. I think that's what it is with classes, people just go to show off what they can do already.

AB So why are you going to pottery classes?

Mam Well, it'll be a way of rubbing shoulders a bit. Then I thought I might try and have a little gathering. Where do you get those little sausages?

AB Who'd come?

Mam The vicar.

AB You don't like the vicar.

Mam I don't dislike him. What I don't like is him trying to rope you in for stuff.

AB Who else?

Mam Well – there's the bank manager.

AB Mam. You've not got a bank. You're in the Post Office Savings.

Mam Well, I could join. You thwart me, you, same as your dad did. You see bank managers in these adverts having amicable discussions with young couples. That's the sort of person. Refined.

AB What would you talk about?

Mam Oh, I'm not short of stuff to talk about – general topics. The environment. Vandalism. The Queen Mother. I've got more strings to my bow than you imagine, you. I thought besides sherry I could serve real coffee. They do it in packets now at Sainsbury's.

AB Mam, you don't like real coffee.

Mam Oh, you. You're always the same. Telling me I ought to get out more, do stuff more, then when I start you go all negative. You're the same as your dad, you. Bless him.

She starts to cry.

AB Nay, Mam.

And so for a time she went to her pottery classes – 'clay night' she used to call it, coming back generally with a stone-age type ashtray she had made – not that anybody in the house smoked.

It's not long after this, though, that the depressions from which she has suffered intermittently over the last ten years become more uninterrupted, the spells in hospital longer, until they merged eventually into a permanent residence in an old people's home in Weston-super-Mare not far from my brother. Here her memory rapidly began to fail but as it failed so her depression begins to lift, leaving her suffused with an unfocused benevolence.

Mam Are we going out?

AB I thought we could just have a little run round.

Mam Well, I shall want my undercoat on.

AB The nurse is fetching it.

Mam They're not nurses, most of them. They're just lasses. You do look bonny.

AB Who am I?

Mam Oh you're . . . you're my son, aren't you?

AB And what's my name?

Mam Ah, now then . . .

She laughs.

AB Here's your coat.

Mam Thank you, love. I've always liked you.

AB And she plants a kiss on the girl's slightly startled cheek. This promiscuous magnanimity extended to things as well as people.

Mam This is nice.

AB What?

Mam This thing you can sit in and go along.

AB The car?

Mam Yes. Oh and what a lovely council estate. She's got her washing out in good time.

AB We have our sandwiches on a hill with a vast view over Somerset. She wants to say what a grand view but her words are going now too.

Mam Oh what a big lot of About.

AB And of some sheep.

Mam You see I know what they are, but I don't know what they're called.

She laughs and it fades.

AB Alas, this general good feeling too had its term and as the years passed she gradually became speechless and beyond communication, though whether she was beyond knowing I could never decide.

I'm not sure this is actually Mrs Bennett's frock.

Nurse Isn't it? Well, I don't think you mind, do you, Lily?

AB And are you sure those are her teeth?

Nurse Oh, I think so. We're actually quite scrupulous about teeth. Only their mouths shrink, you know.

AB Nor was it just her frock or her teeth. She had lost even her name.

Nurse She's lovely is Lily, isn't she?

AB Her name is Lilian actually.

Nurse Yes, only we call her Lily, don't we, Lily? Give us a kiss then. That's a good girl.

AB Babies like my nephew and niece's children she could still respond to, babble at them as they babbled at her. And I suspect she would have been able to talk to a cat if cats had been allowed. But babies and cats, things to stroke and pet, are not part of the accoutrements of homes for the aged.

Kissing was the last thing to go. I would purse my lips and she would do the same without knowing who I was or what I was doing, fetching my face up to hers. But she would kiss it.

In time, though, the kissing stopped and there was only being kissed and if you were good like my brother you would talk to her. But wanting any response or a sign that she knew what talking was – or what indeed I was, this thing that loomed periodically at the side of her bed.

So I would sit there for an hour every fortnight holding her hand, now as thin and transparent as an anatomical drawing; every vein you could see.

Once in a café she said, 'This tea tastes like octopus pee,' burst out laughing, saying 'I've given you some script,' meaning, I imagine, all the phrases she came out with and her silliness and her jokes.

She was right. Only there didn't have to be words. Some of the best script she gives me is when speech has entirely forsaken her and she is lying in that upper room overlooking the sands and sounds of Weston-super-Mare as another long afternoon draws to its close and she drifts between sleeping and waking and living and dying, month after month, year upon year.

A silent script it is, a motionless movie as I sit recollecting our lives.

The tide comes in, lapping thinly over the sand but never enough to float her off and carry her away.

Mam Did you find your childhood?

AB Not really.

Mam Will it be me that's got it?

AB No.

Mam It'll be like everything else. Your dad will have wuthered it.

She laughs.

Him playing the fiddle. Is that childhood?

AB It is now. Though it didn't seem so then.

What I cannot explain to my mother, and scarcely to myself, is I have come to see that I know more than I think I know and that, however sparse and seemingly unserviceable my memories, this doesn't matter because you don't put yourself into what you write, you find yourself there. And for a writer the life you don't have is as ample a territory as the life that you do.

Sound of a party.

Man Did she just die, Aunty Lilian?

AB Yes. She slept away. Well, she was ninety-one.

Man I hadn't seen her since your dad's funeral. This is nice sherry.

AB Yes. I found it in the cupboard. It must be twenty years old.

Man Vintage! They were both teetotallers, weren't they?

AB Not by conviction. It just didn't agree with them.

Man I wish it didn't agree with me!

Woman It's a grand do you've put on. These sausages are lovely.

AB They come from M&S. They do all that now, I hadn't realised – sausages on sticks, canapés, dips . . . cream cheese enrobed in smoked salmon. Party food. It must never have been easier to have a function.

Woman That's right. In your mam's day it would have been Shippam's fish paste. Mind you, they weren't keen on parties, were they?

AB No. But the vicar's here and the doctor and some neighbours and what remains of our relations. People are standing up and talking rather than sitting down and some are having coffee and some are having sherry. So in the end she got what she wanted: a cocktail party.
 When it came to my turn I, who never thought much of cocktails, am being given them too at regular intervals.

Doctor We shall be giving you a sophisticated cocktail of drugs over about six months.

AB My cocktail comes not in a shallow glass, and with no cherry on a stick, still less a Japanese umbrella. Mine comes in a bag, a transparent udder that drips toxicants (though not intoxicants) into me during a two-day binge every fortnight. From time to time the bag is shaken though not stirred by the cocktail waitress, whose name today is Caitlin, who is from Galway, her sister also a sister but in the Princess Grace Hospital, Abu Dhabi.

Doctor You may feel a little tired, but hopefully nothing else.

AB Some people are nauseated by it but there are pills for that now, though none for the boredom of it and the wearisomeness.

Irish Nurse How are we doing? Oh, won't be long now.

AB But it is long. Two and a half days it takes, and afterwards I feel heavy, jet-lagged almost.
 It's like every two weeks I fly to Australia. But all that was fifteen years ago. So – take heart.

Some Ivor Novello on a single violin.

THE NATIONAL THEATRE

The National Theatre, where this play had its premiere, is central to the creative life of the UK. In its three theatres on the South Bank in London it presents an eclectic mix of new plays and classics from the world repertoire, with seven or eight productions in repertory at any one time. And through an extensive programme of amplifying activities – Platform performances, backstage tours, foyer music, publications, exhibitions and outdoor events – it recognises that theatre doesn't begin and end with the rise and fall of the curtain.

The National endeavours to maintain and re-energise the great traditions of the British stage and to expand the horizons of audiences and artists alike. It aspires to reflect in its repertoire the diversity of the nation's culture. It takes a particular responsibility for the creation of new work – offering at the NT Studio a space for research and development for the NT's stages and the theatre as a whole. Through its Learning Programme, it invites people of all ages to discover the NT's repertoire, the skills and excitement of theatre-making, and the building itself. As the national theatre, it aims to foster the health of the wider British theatre through policies of collaboration and touring. These activities demonstrate the considerable public benefit provided by the NT, both locally and nationally.

Between 20 and 26 new productions are staged each year in one of the NT's three theatres, the Olivier, the Lyttelton and the Cottesloe. In 2011–12, the National's total reach was 2.3 million people worldwide, through attendances on the South Bank, in the West End, on tour and through National Theatre Live, the digital broadcast of live performances to cinema screens all over the world.

Information: +44(0) 20 7452 3400
Box Office: +44(0) 20 7452 3000
National Theatre, South Bank, London SE1 9PX
www.nationaltheatre.org.uk`
Registered Charity No: 224223